Trade in Services

Trade in Services

A Case for Open Markets

Jonathan David Aronson and
Peter F. Cowhey

American Enterprise Institute for Public Policy Research
Washington and London

Jonathan David Aronson is associate professor, School of International Relations, University of Southern California. Peter F. Cowhey is associate professor of political science, University of California at San Diego.

We thank Sven Arndt, Claude Barfield, and Jeffrey Schott for their comments.

J.D.A./P.F.C.

To order call toll free 1-800-462-6420 or 1-717-794-3800. For all other inquiries please contact the AEI Press, 1150 Seventeenth Street, N.W., Washington, D.C. 20036 or call 1-800-862-5801.

Aronson, Jonathan David.
 Trade in services.

 1. Service industries. 2. Service industries—United States. I. Cowhey, Peter F., 1948–   . II. Title.
HD9980.5.A66 1984   382'.45'000973   84-72731
ISBN 0-8447-3570-1

1 3 5 7 9 10 8 6 4 2

AEI Studies 415

Contents

Introduction

The architects of the world trade system largely ignored the service sector for three decades. But during the past two decades, the trade in services has become an important source of jobs and economic growth. In 1980 global service exports totaled about $370 billion, approximately 20 percent of world trade. Still, no coherent system of rules, principles, and procedures exists to govern trade in services. Furthermore, multilateral trade negotiations did not even consider services until Tokyo Round negotiations of the mid-1970s, and then only at the insistence of the United States. Since then, however, the United States has pushed for more attention for trade in services. U.S. persistence has begun to reap results. Trade in services was one of the three most debated issues at the November 1982 General Agreement on Tariffs and Trade (GATT) ministerial meeting, and the May 1983 Williamsburg Summit's closing statement included a commitment to work toward free trade in services.

The increased attention to trade in services raises several important questions for the U.S. government. This paper concentrates on three of them. First, given the wide range of pressing trade problems, do services merit such a prominent place in the trade agenda of the United States; or have American diplomats once again become obsessed with the novel at the expense of more critical trade issues? Second, even if services deserve a high priority in principle, is it feasible to negotiate general rules for the services trade under GATT? Are other countries willing to change their longstanding history of regulation of services markets and to expose their national firms to the challenges of large U.S. service firms? Third, if freer trade in services is possible, what lessons does a theory of the politics of free trade suggest about how to pursue this objective? If the United States enters into multilateral negotiations on services, what might it expect to achieve?

Our answer to the first question (What is the national interest?) emerges in chapters 1 and 2. We argue that the rationalization of the services sector will yield important efficiency gains for the United States and world economy. An emphasis on services complements a policy to maintain a healthy industrial sector. Chapter 3 answers our second question (Is GATT a feasible framework for a negotiation on

1

services?) by demonstrating that GATT is an adequate, albeit imperfect, vehicle to work out the partial deregulation of national services. Chapter 4 addresses the third question (What political guidelines should govern service negotiations?) by arguing that the new rules must control risks and provide a limited "safety net" for countries accepting freer trade in services.

1
The Role of Services

The "service economy" is a somewhat amorphous concept. It governs various activities that do not neatly fit together except that they are not manufactured and commodity goods. Therefore, before we analyze the options for government policy, we summarize the basic facts about services in world trade and the U.S. economy.

Definitions and Statistics

Analysts treat services as a residual category that includes all output not originating from the goods-producing sectors: agriculture, mining, manufacturing, and construction.[1] Categorization is difficult because many goods-producing activities compose a large and growing service component, as we shall explain later. Moreover, some services, such as construction/engineering, are neither fish nor fowl, being involved with the production of goods and of services.

In the absence of a more precise definition, the service sector is usually specified in terms of lists. Thus service activities might include the items in table 1.

Services, whether in national or international commerce, are also notoriously difficult to measure.[2] But their fundamental importance for the U.S. economy is indisputable. Services are critical for the U.S. economy for three reasons. They constitute the largest share of gross national product (GNP) and employment. Moreover, services promise to regenerate growing productivity in the economy as they become more technologically sophisticated and capital intensive. Finally, they are an increasingly critical component of what we traditionally have classified as the manufacturing and goods sectors.

The percentage of the U.S. GNP produced within the service sector has grown steadily since World War II. In 1948, $140 billion (54 percent) of the $260 billion U.S. GNP was accounted for by services. In 1981, the U.S. service sector contributed $1.95 trillion of the almost $3 trillion U.S. GNP. The same pattern is found in other industrial countries. They are increasing everywhere.[3]

The growing share of services in the economy does not mean that

3

TABLE 1
TYPES OF SERVICES

Travel, Transportation, Tourism, and Leisure Services
Lodging
Recreational and cultural services
Shipping (freight)
Tourism (tourist counseling, tour operating)
Transport of goods (air, rail, road, inland waterways, but excluding ocean
    transport)
Travel (passenger transport)

Return on Capital
Factor income (direct and other investment income)
Licensing (royalties, license fees, copyrights, and other forms of property
    income excluding income from financial assets)
Rental (real estate)
Workers' remittances

Support Services
Accounting
Advertising
Education
Personal services (for example, domestics, drivers, hairdressers)
Professional services (consultant, economic, legal, medical, and technical)
Repairs and maintenance

Construction/Engineering Services
Construction and engineering (project execution, design management
    training, and consulting)

Telecommunications, Information, and Data-Processing Services
Data processing (computer treatment of information bases)
Motion pictures, printing, and art work
Telecommunications (telephone, telegraph, television, tele-data
    transmission)

Financial and Insurance Services
Banking and other financial services
Brokerage (transport and insurance)
Insurance and reinsurance

TABLE 1 *(Continued)*

Management Services

Employment
Franchising, chartering
Health (such as hospital management)
Leasing
Wholesaling and retailing

SOURCE: Author's reclassification of various studies on services. Examples of such sources include: Harley L. Browning and Joachim Singelmann, "The Transformation of the U.S. Labor Force: The Interaction of Industry and Occupation," *Politics and Society*, vol. 8, no. 3–4 (1978), pp. 481–509; Thomas M. Stanback, Jr., et al., *Services in the New Economy* (Totowa, N.J.: Allanheld, Osmun, & Co., 1981); Neil L. McKellar, "A Classification of Services for International Trade Report to Task Force on Trade in Services," Ottawa, March 1982, pp. 1–7, cited in Robert M. Stern, "Global Dimensions and Determinants of International Trade and Investment in Services," paper presented at the 3rd Annual Workshop on U.S.-Canadian Relations (Current Issues in Trade and Investment in Service Industries: U.S.-Canadian Bilateral and Multilateral Perspectives), Ann Arbor, Michigan, October 19–20, 1984, appendix A.

the United States is becoming a nation engaged in making Mc-Donald's hamburgers as its primary products. The growth includes the vastly increased expenditures for social services such as health. More significantly, every good produced requires a growing measure of data and other services as an input to production.[4]

Furthermore, the growing role of services in producing goods does not mean productivity will decrease. The proportion of jobs within traditional service sectors (such as the preparation of goods, household labor, and health care) has held steady at about 10 percent. Information jobs (such as programming, writing, secretarial work, accountancy, law, and banking) have grown to roughly 50 percent of U.S. jobs. This share, according to Charles Jonscher, should have almost peaked, because greater capital investment in services is raising productivity steadily. This rise will significantly bolster aggregate national productivity. U.S. government estimates indicate that by 1982 investments in new technology for services reached $47 billion per annum. Those estimates indicate that almost half of the thirty most capital-intensive industries are in the service sector.[5]

In summary, services constitute a large share of the U.S. economy. Therefore, efficiency in the production and use of services has important implications for national productivity. While technological advances and larger capital spending are providing significant improvements along these lines, the benefits of more efficient international commerce in services are not trivial. Trade and foreign investment are two traditional mechanisms for enhancing national and international welfare.

Trade and the Service Sector

Here we focus on data on trade in services and income from fees and royalties. *We exclude data on income earned on foreign assets and official transactions from our analysis.* These other figures, although included in the U.S. Invisibles Account, cloud rather than clarify the analysis because they mix trade with investment.[6] The most striking aspect about what remains is that internationally, between 1970 and 1980, the average annual compound growth rate of service exports (18.7 percent) lagged behind the growth rate of merchandise exports (20.4 percent). All of these growth rates, however, exceeded the growth in global gross domestic product (14.2 percent).[7] Therefore, the international trade in services is becoming a growing share of total world output, but it is doing so less rapidly than goods are.

The International Monetary Fund (IMF) estimates that in 1980 the value of global services exports reached about $370 billion, probably about 20 percent of world trade. The United States, the largest exporter of services, sold $37.5 billion in services abroad, about 10 percent of the total. The European community exported about five times as many services as the United States. At the national level, the United Kingdom exported $37.1 billion; West Germany, $33.8 billion; France, $33.0 billion; Italy, $23.5 billion; Japan, $19.4 billion; the Netherlands, $18.6 billion; Belgium, $14.9 billion; Spain, $12.2 billion; and Austria, $10.8 billion. These top ten service exporting countries accounted for about two-thirds of total global service exports in 1980. The top twenty-five service exporters accounted for 87 percent of the total. The top twenty-five included Mexico (13th), Singapore (16th), South Korea (17th), Saudi Arabia (20th), and Egypt (25th).[8]

The aggregate figures on exports mask a more important factor—the mix between more traditional services (such as tourism and transport) and those involving significant new skills and technological advantages. Although the statistics do not permit precise disaggregation, U.S. government studies and policy papers on the services industry provide a fairly consistent picture of the mix of service exports. The portrait makes one wonder why American officials are eager to liberalize trade in services. In 1980 the $37.5 billion of U.S. service exports consisted largely of travel, passenger fares and transportation plus approximately $10.8 billion for other private services including fees and royalties. Over half of this last figure comes from fees and

TABLE 2
SERVICE EXPORTS IN THE U.S. BALANCE OF PAYMENTS, 1980
(billions of U.S. dollars)

	Receipts	Net Balance
Travel	9.985	−.399
Passenger fares	2.582	−.951
Other transportation	11.041	.060
Fees and royalties	6.993	6.236
Other private services	4.645	1.665
Subtotal private services	35.246	6.611
Income on investment	56.689	31.544
Total for services and investment income	91.935	38.155
Total for all goods	284.198	−27.354

SOURCE: Economic Consulting Services, *The International Operations of U.S. Service Industries: Current Data Collection and Analysis* (June 1981), p. 8.

royalties from affiliated and unaffiliated foreigners. Thus the direct sale of technologically sophisticated services may account for as little as $5 billion of overall U.S. service sales. Most information and other technologically sophisticated services are counted as "other private services" in table 2. Some also fall under "fees and royalties." As a percentage of total service exports this figure compares unfavorably with the record of other countries.[9]

Obviously, a disparity exists between the intuition of American policy makers that services have been driven by U.S. strengths in information and financial skills and the U.S. trade statistics. A more careful analysis of the data suggest that intuition has been a better guide than the official statistics.

An important study by the Economic Consulting Services, Inc., has argued persuasively that world trade in services is undercounted.[10] ECS advocated excluding investment incomes from direct foreign investment from the service accounts but suggested that the figures on investment income are disguising revenues from foreign services. Buried in the returns on investment was a substantial volume of trade in services because there was no appropriate way to list them under conventional statistical reporting systems. Instead of

TABLE 3
ESTIMATED FOREIGN REVENUES OF THE U.S. SERVICE SECTOR, 1980

Service Industry	Billions of U.S. Dollars
Accounting	2.35
Advertising	2.05
Banking	9.10
Business/professional/technical services	1.07
Construction/engineering	5.36
Education	1.27
Employment	0.55
Franchising	1.26
Health	0.27
Information	0.60
Insurance	6.00
Leasing	2.35
Lodging	4.60
Motion pictures	1.14
Tourism	4.15
Transportation	13.93
Subtotal, 16 industries	56.05
Total for all U.S. services	60.0

SOURCE: ECS, *International Operations*, p. 294.

$37.5 billion in foreign trade receipts, the United States earned $60 billion in 1980, of which roughly $56 billion was in sixteen major categories. More important, whereas conventional accounting made travel and transport about two-thirds of services income, this estimate reduced them to 38 percent of the total. Therefore, it is easier to see why services are major growth prospects for the United States (see table 3). The receipts on financial services trading (banking and insurance) was $15.1 billion. The revenues from professional and information services (as classified in table 1) was $13.3 billion, and leasing and franchising arrangements provided $3.7 billion.

The figures on revenues do not show how much the United States earned on its net trade balance for each category. We cannot easily fill in the gap because no one has done an analysis of international payments by the United States for services that is equivalent to the ECS revision of 1980 international receipts. But a crude comparison of 1979 payments (about $20.3 billion) with 1979 estimated reve-

TABLE 4
GROSS RECEIPTS FROM FOREIGN OPERATIONS FOR U.S. SERVICE FIRMS
(billions of U.S. dollars)

Service Industry	Total Worldwide (including U.S.)	Foreign
Accounting[a]	7.99	1.96
Advertising[b]	27.761	10.414
Banking[c]	—	46.8
	1,363.00[d]	290.0 [d]
Business services:		
Management and consulting[e]	10.10	0.75
Legal[e]	27.83	0.278
Technical[e]	18.86	0.047
Construction/engineering[f]	113.0	49.08
Employment/franchising/leasing[g]	332.95	15.99
Information[h]	9.00	0.428
	1.854[i]	0.213[i]
Insurance[j]	—	10.957

NOTE: Dash = not available.

a. 1977 figures.

b. 1980 billings.

c. 1980 interest received on overseas assets and other international clients.

d. 1980 total assets.

e. 1980 estimated.

f. 1980 global contract awards for top 400 construction firms and 1980 foreign construction, construction management and design awards for all U.S. firms.

g. 1980 sales of foreign franchise units (includes some employment and leasing).

h. 1979 total revenues for all firms.

i. 1979 total revenues for leading firms.

j. 1980 net book value of equity and loans for foreign affiliates.

SOURCE: Computed by authors from data in ECS, *International Operations*, pp. 70, 76, 88, 103, 113, 126, 158, 174, and 194.

nues (about $23 billion) suggests that the United States ran a deficit on travel, tourism, and transport of $2.7 billion.[11] The surplus for all services might be $20 billion, however, if we assign about half of investment receipts and payments to the service category.[12] Both the volume of surplus and the sources of the yield suggest a far more exciting future for the service trade than do the official estimates.

Our review of trade performance has demonstrated three points. First, trade in services is not swamping the trade in goods even though it constitutes a growing share of the world's GNP. Trade in services complements and facilitates trade in goods. Second, service exports are highly concentrated in the hands of roughly twenty-five nations. The United States is by no means highly dominant. Third, the competitive strengths of the United States are probably in the higher technology and financial services, but the official trade figures do not accurately reflect these advantages. The next section explains why these strengths also are dependent on the overseas expansion of U.S. service firms.

Efficiency and the Internationalization of Services

An analysis of services in the world economy relying only on trade data fundamentally underestimates the international commerce in services and, therefore, the efficiency gains from rationalizing the sector. A service company might now operate in many nations. We shall call the process of producing and distributing a good or a service through local subsidiaries, affiliates, or franchises the *internationalization* of the industry. Trade data do not fully reflect the magnitude of this process because much of the local production and distribution does not cross national boundaries.[13]

Most theories explaining the rise of the vertically integrated firm and the multinational corporation now agree that they are the products of imperfections in the market (such as large economies of scale) or the costs of negotiating and implementing contracts.[14]

Just as there are economies of scale in the efficient provision of goods, there are economies of scale in the provision of services. Ten small banks spread around the globe cannot provide the same efficiency of service to a global customer as can Citibank. A need for local service providers, however, will always exist because they have specialized knowledge of the local market and because no international firm will rely exclusively on a single provider of a key service. Therefore, the internationalization of the service industry will never consist exclusively of giant service firms following Fortune 500 companies around the world.

Also, services are highly sensitive to the particular needs of customers. Most services require extensive investment in specialized personal relations and data-sharing arrangements by both the provider and the user. As a result, both parties suffer if government rules arbitrarily force them to limit their relationship to only a few types of transactions. Moreover, because many services are highly regulated, the service firms operate in many countries to offer a variety of products made possible by diverse regulatory systems (such as occurs with many offshore banking units). Thus the costs of information and bar-

10

gaining to providers and users lead to internationalization in the provision of services. As with conventional economies of scale there are significant efficiency gains from this development.

It is difficult to know to what extent various services have become internationalized. But we can begin to see the magnitude of foreign revenues (that is, money earned outside the home country) in relation to trade revenues by comparing tables 3 and 4. Table 4 presents alternative measures of total foreign revenues for selected U.S. industries. The figures reflect gross receipts, not the net (that is, after expenses) receipts, of the foreign operations of U.S. firms. (In some cases the figures represent assets or contract awards.) Table 4 shows only industries in which existing data allow an alternative calculation of gross foreign receipts to the data reported in table 3.

For advertising, banking, and construction/engineering, the net foreign revenues reported in table 3 were, respectively, $2.05 billion, $9.10 billion, and $5.36 billion. Table 4 uses alternative measures for the three industries of total billings to clients, interest and other income from foreign operations, and total foreign receipts from projects. If one uses these figures, receipts soar to, respectively, $10.4 billion, $46.8 billion, and $49.1 billion—sums five to ten times larger than those reported in table 3.

Table 4 suggests two important conclusions about the world services economy. First, national units of production and distribution play a smaller role in the production and distribution of services than an examination of trade figures would reveal. Although firms from the United States may differ from those from other countries because they have more foreign investments, this analysis applies to non-U.S. service firms as well. Therefore, we suggest that *net foreign trade is small, but the service sector's production and distribution is becoming highly internationalized.* This conclusion is important because in the past national production always dominated the service sector. Countries can no longer choose whether or not to permit the internationalization of the service sector.

Our second conclusion is that in rapidly growing, increasingly internationalized service sectors, the size and the scale of a country's firms are important attributes of its competitive position in the world market. In many services the fate of U.S. industry leaders depends largely on their foreign revenues. For example, the same data used to create table 4 indicate that the "Big Eight" accounting firms earned one-third of their revenues from foreign billings and the top ten advertising agencies derive more than 50 percent of their revenues from overseas. The largest fifty information-processing service firms earned 11.5 percent of their proceeds outside the United States, while

11

annual contract awards for U.S. engineering/construction firms from international sources in 1980 ran at 30 percent. Banks had 20 percent of all their assets in foreign branches, and this figure was much higher for the largest banks. At the other end of the spectrum, business, technical, and professional services (including management-consulting and law firms) derived only 1.8 percent of their sales outside the United States. In short, the degree of dependence varies sharply, but foreign revenues are crucial for many firms if they are to maintain the scale and breadth of experience necessary to be competitive.

2

Trade Imperfections and Economies of Scale: Implications for U.S. Firms

Many observers think of trade in services as the last refuge for industrial and academic scalawags: the U.S. priority for services is a measure to hide the bankruptcy of its industrial policy. This section clarifies the U.S. interest in the world service market. It begins by presenting the skeptics' case against trade in services as a priority and then shows the basis for affirming it as a priority.

The Case against Services as a Priority

The first set of critics of liberalized trade in services argues that the United States already dominates the world service market and that it would be the chief beneficiary of liberalization. According to this logic, the dollar's role as the key currency, the U.S. role as the institutional center of the world economy, and the U.S. position as the world's largest market gives the United States an insurmountable advantage in the world service trade, especially the financial service market. The tone of the arguments surrounding services was pithily captured by one analyst:

> By the mid 1960s, the key American export shifted again, to financial services and dollars, as big American banks extended overseas and supplied dollar credits that other countries needed to play in the big leagues of international trade. When Richard Nixon cut the link between gold and the dollar in 1972, he removed limits on the growth rate of dollar holdings overseas . . . and the American export industries settled semipermanently into selling financial services and dollars on the one hand, and farm products on the other. Dollars are a product that the government, not industry, manufactures. America's position as a food exporter owes as much to providence . . . as it does to the intrinsic efficiency

13

of farmers. Neither of our bellwether exports has much to do with the competitiveness of American businessmen.[15]

According to the critics, the advantages of financial leadership are only one part of the U.S. edge. The early dominance of the U.S. multinational corporation also established this country's service firms as the dominant international forces in the sector. Because these firms now enjoy large economies of scale and advantages in transaction costs, other countries, especially developing nations, cannot expect their firms to become competitive. For example, the following is a Canadian commentary on U.S. policy about the trade in transborder data flows:

> The notion of free flow [of transborder data] becomes an obfuscation for that of free trade. And developing economies know well that free trade is the slogan of hegemonic, imperial economies. . . . The United States has been resisting any efforts to restrict the transborder flow of data on grounds of national sovereignty, public order, or national security. In effect, the American goal is to stop foreign governments from making policy on TBDF so that the American market's superior mass will attract data processing to it.[16]

A second set of critics (primarily of U.S. origin) takes a different line. These critics argue that the United States may repeat the economic errors of Britain. In this view the United Kingdom's lagging performance in the world economy is a product of the financial preferences of the "City of London." For many years Britain chose to protect the exchange rate value of sterling to promote its role as the hub of international financial services. The price of this decision was periodic bouts of deflation at home (so-called stop and go politics) and a general inattentiveness to the needs of merchandise exporters. Over the long run, even its leadership in financial services became weak because of the erosion in the industrial base.

For these critics the parallel to the United States is fairly clear. By trial and error the U.S. government is slowly moving to policies that maintain a strong dollar at the expense of industrial exports and to the benefit of the growth of New York as the world financial hub. The new initiative to liberalize trade in services is yet another mistaken priority because it wastes valuable political capital on services rather than promoting goods.[17]

In short, the attack on services as an economic priority rests on two strands of argument. First, the United States is pursuing this policy only because of a dominant position based on unfair advantages. Second, it is not wise to give services pride of place before

14

goods in economic or trade policy. In our view the second line of attack is more cogent than the first, but it should be treated more as a caution than as a tenet for policy.

We believe that the first line of attack is mistaken about the facts and confused about the sources of U.S. advantages. As our analysis has demonstrated, U.S. leadership in the service trade is hardly overwhelming. And, although the United States has done reasonably well in some of the traditional services, it is also common to hear suspicions of unfair advantages for U.S. firms in many of the newer services.

One possible reason for the preeminence of American service companies is that they are based in the world's largest, most powerful market system. American firms profit from their huge domestic market, attractive capital markets, technological leadership, close ties to U.S. multinationals, and deregulation of domestic markets that have spurred new products. Certainly they also have profited from the political leverage of the United States in writing the rules for commercial diplomacy.

The advantages for U.S. firms are sufficiently great to give pause to other countries. As our data indicated, however, most industrial countries already are substantial exporters of services. At least for these nations, the provision of services is not intrinsically different from that of goods.

Technical knowledge diffuses, and the market usually grows large enough for many competitors to achieve substantial economies of scale. Bankers and investors also become more willing to finance new entrants. As barriers to entry for new competitors crumble, competition expands. This process is as true of insurance, banking, and the management of hospitals for profit as it is of computers and cars. Besides, as we will elaborate shortly, different countries have competitive advantages in different segments of a given service at the same time.

The large economies of scale available to local operations in Europe, Japan, and North America do not apply as readily to the developing countries. Here the traditional arguments on behalf of infant industries—the necessity of restricting imports to build economies of scale for local industry—may apply for services. One might further argue, unlike manufacturing and commodities, that the international political community has not yet dedicated adequate resources to assist the third world in becoming more competitive in these businesses.

From the perspective of developing countries, free trade is particularly suspect because their principal gains in these markets have occurred as a result of barriers to competition. In particular, the conventions governing traffic in airlines, shipping, and telecommunications guarantee that these countries will receive some minimum share of revenues from transactions involving their countries.

The chief danger of such a protectionist stance is that the infant industry may become a senior statesman of society. For example, a classic problem of import substitution industrialization in Latin America was the growth of privileged firms that never became internationally competitive. They acquired vast political influence, however. They often had first claims on such scarce resources as foreign exchange. Today restrictions on competition in services could make some firms the special beneficiaries of crucial international services such as information and telecommunications. (Those firms might, for example, have first call on a limited number of phone lines allotted to a foreign data bank.)

If necessary, developing countries should adopt protectionist measures for infant service industries that are easily identifiable and should include a predetermined schedule for the elimination of those measures. Perhaps most importantly, if developing countries choose to protect industries at home, they also need more discriminating policies about when and which foreign firms can enter their markets as investors.

So far our review of claims of unfair U.S. advantages has suggested that the issue is more pertinent to firms of developing nations. Nonetheless, one remaining advantage shapes the behavior of *all* parties in the world market. Financial, technical, and general commercial barriers to entry ought to decline, but government regulations that obstruct entry may prove more durable. The very barriers to a liberal service trade that hamper U.S. competitors produce the worst of both worlds: they lead both to inefficiency and to protectionism, and they reinforce the domination of U.S. firms.

U.S. services traditionally followed the flag of U.S. clients overseas. While most countries tried to accommodate this expansion to remain attractive to foreign investment (and to receive the advantages provided by some U.S. services), they also tried to limit the deluge. Restrictions, over time, created an informal and imprecise allocation of the total market share of all foreign firms as a group. Because U.S. firms were sometimes the first and usually the largest entrants into foreign markets after World War II, many of them acquired a "grandfathered" position within the foreign share of the market. In many services, such as data communications, those grandfathered include local subsidiaries or partners of U.S. companies. The result is that U.S. firms are retarded in their growth but effective new competition by third parties is severely hindered. For example, a recent Organiza-

16

tion for Economic Cooperation and Development (OECD) question-naire showed no U.S. firms reporting serious problems arising from European privacy provisions but many European firms complaining that they were hampered by their neighbors' practices.[18]

To summarize, U.S. firms are somewhat hindered in competing by restrictions on trade in services. But, with the British, they had early market leadership; therefore, restrictions hurt potential global competitors more than they hurt U.S. firms. Thus the economies of scale and the knowledge of local markets that have traditionally strengthened U.S. firms are reinforced by retarding the entry of others.

The Case for Services as a Priority

As a rule of thumb, liberalization will produce temporary gains for U.S. firms involved with technologically sophisticated services, be-cause those firms will be free to exploit their comparative advantages fully. Liberalization, however, will also make foreign firms more com-petitive with U.S. firms that provide "smokestack" services.[19]

One might ask: Is it not therefore in the U.S. interest to keep a restricted market? Our answer is no. To have its firms misallocate resources because of serious market imperfections is never in the long-term interest of the United States or any other country. If the leadership of U.S. corporations depends on barriers to entry due to trade restrictions, then the firms are receiving a false message from the market about the efficient allocation of scarce resources. Grand-fathering, another means of restricting entry into the market, may help a few U.S. companies but restrict the overall market share for all U.S. firms. This point is crucial to rebutting the worries of those who fear that the United States will sacrifice its industrial base to promote services. We would argue that, assuming a continued commitment to efficiency, the service initiative would benefit U.S. manufacturing as well as service industries, the U.S. trade position, and international welfare.

The benefits for industry occur because the United States has irrevocably decided (at least in the medium-term) to deregulate many services. Liberalization of trade in services, therefore, is now crucial to the protection of U.S. producers of goods because service companies are among the largest purchasers of high-technology goods, as is shown, for example, by the immense equipment procurement by phone companies. When the United States deregulated services and other countries did not do so as thoroughly, U.S. equipment firms faced a new risk. They could lose sales to foreign competitors in the U.S. market without having equal access to regulated service suppliers elsewhere. The only way to correct this imbalance is to encourage liberalization in competition regarding all facets of the service trade. (The argument for reciprocity as a substitute for liberalization is discussed in chapter 4.)

Moreover, free trade in services will permit more extensive rationalization of the world services sector. As chapter 1 showed, services are a growing component of the costs of goods. They also are an important determinant of which strategies are feasible for global production and distribution of goods.[20] All of the traditional arguments on behalf of free trade as an efficiency maximizer apply strongly to the relation of trade in services to the production of goods. Liberalization would also yield gains in trade for both the United States and other countries.

The advantages for the United States in trading services more freely do not imply severe losses for other countries. In fact, the classic model of national comparative advantages divided by industry applies less aptly than the newer models of intra-industry specialization in trade. According to this latter model, countries do not trade stereos for shoes. They exchange shoe laces and turntables for shoe soles and stereo speakers. Freer trade allows all players to exploit economies of scale. (This statement implies that the lower prices resulting from more competition may be offset by reduced costs.) In addition, firms will specialize in particular niches to build scale economies and will defend their position by reputation for quality, by name brand recognition, and by distributional advantages that are roughly consistent with Chamberlain models of monopolistic competition.[21] Intra-industry specialization also reduces the risks for any country from freer trade because most industries do not collapse because of foreign competition. Rather, on the average, they adjust in size and in specialization. For example, the deregulation of financial services has spurred many subspecializations. While large institutions strive to cover the spectrum, the market also has room for many new specialists.

Our review of the case against services demonstrated several flaws in the argument. "Unfair" U.S. advantages may be a function of current restrictions on trade imposed by other countries. More competition through freer trade would benefit all. Besides, given deregulation in the United States and the growing role of services in the production of goods, the attempt to liberalize trade in services complements rather than undercuts a policy to revitalize the manufacturing sector. And the internationalization of services has made the welfare losses from inefficiency a serious common concern for all countries.

Serious objections about the political feasibility of increased competition in many countries and the applicability of GATT rules remain (see chapter 3). Nonetheless, the trends outlined here are beginning to influence negotiations. At the GATT ministerial meeting in November 1982, the United States encountered considerable opposition from the developing countries, led by India and Brazil but joined by others, to the service initiative. Europe was lukewarm at best, and the French and Italians were quite cool. Surprisingly, the Spanish, who ran the third largest service trade surplus in 1981 and 1982 and ran larger surpluses than the United States in the three previous years, sided with the developing countries in opposing the services liberalization initiative. Canada, Australia, and Japan were moderately supportive but cautioned restraint. Most of the contracting parties were doubtful about undertaking a major effort to liberalize trade in services while the global recession was fanning protectionist claims. There was also considerable suspicion that the United States knew something that others did not know and thus could not be trusted and a belief that there had not been adequate preparation and international coordination on services before the meeting.

In October 1983 sentiments seemed to change somewhat. After looking at the data, Ambassador Tran, trade negotiator and chief of the European Community's Geneva delegation, stated "we are convinced that we must have an international discipline if we want to secure and expand trade in services. . . . The homework since the ministerial (meeting) has made us convinced that it is in our interests" to have guidelines on service sector trade.[22] A week later Leslie Fielding, the EC's director general of external relations, indicated support for some liberalization or, at least, for no new measures of protectionism. He suggested that the first step toward a negotiation on trade in services could come at the GATT annual meeting in November 1984.[23] About the same time the developing countries tempered their criticism of involvement by the GATT secretariat on service issues, promising to allow some attention to services in the GATT.[24] Although they prefer a forum deemed more congenial to their interests, the developing countries are not exempt from the political forces favoring more competition.

3
Deregulation and the GATT System

Irrespective of the importance of the global service industry, placing it high on the trade agenda may still be imprudent. Freer trade in services does not require that other countries match the ardor of the United States for deregulation of domestic service markets. Some leeway for greater competition is necessary, however. Even if such a change in domestic policies is feasible, perhaps GATT is not an apt model for guiding international commerce in services.

Chapter 3 examines both problems. It concludes that some deregulation of competition in major countries is likely and the GATT rules could work even with a modest opening. Also, if a more thorough overhaul of trade rules is possible, GATT can serve as an adequate, albeit untidy, guide for reform.

Deregulation

Services in the United States are supplied by private individuals and firms. Since the mid-1970s the United States has fostered increased competition through deregulation in the aviation, trucking, telecommunications, and financial sectors. This deregulatory thrust also allowed many U.S. service firms to compete more actively overseas. At the same time deregulation allowed foreign service providers more access to the U.S. market. In contrast, most other countries provide key services through government-owned or government-controlled monopolies and firms. Although Britain, Canada, Australia, and Japan have shown some interest in privatizing and deregulating in specific service sectors, there remains a problem of how to organize fair and free competition for services internationally. No country can impose its regulatory philosophy on another. The question is whether, given these differences, discussions and negotiations designed to promote free trade in services can succeed. In short, are the problems that prevent free trade in services solvable, and are countries ready to solve them?

The U.S. preference for open competition among private firms in the market has roots in the unique political tradition of the United States. Other countries, with different traditions, feel no need or desire to emulate the U.S. competitive model. As a result, the recent U.S. push for deregulation may not herald impending changes elsewhere. The *political* logic that supported strong regulation of the service businesses, however, may be beginning to crumble in many nations. Deregulation and privatization would not automatically lead to freer trade in services, but it might stimulate more open international competition. In addition, technological advances have altered the nature of many regulated industries and made it more difficult to enforce regulations in some instances.

Long ago most governments assumed responsibility for the independent provision of key services involving large economies of scale (such as telecommunication, mail, and water) or strictly limited the right of outsiders to enter and compete in the provision of services (such as air, inland water, and truck transportation). The original economic rationale for state control has eroded in some areas, such as telecommunications, and was never really appropriate in other services, such as trucking. Nonetheless, consumers usually favored government regulation even when prices were higher than necessary. As long as inflation remained low, individual and corporate consumers cared more about reliability and quality of services than about prices.[25] Not only did consumers pay a premium to ensure an adequate, timely supply of services, they also supported limitations on entry into competition. For this reason and because it was (and is) difficult and expensive for consumers to judge the quality of services provided, consumers often were willing to restrict competition to ensure quality. (Typically, service industries or professional associations require service suppliers to meet technical, performance, and safety standards.)

In the formative years of modern industrial society, regulation also promoted the universal extension of some "merit services" which yield large positive externalities—particularly telephone, transport, and health. When key services were first introduced, cross-subsidies made this extension possible. In some cases, one service (for example, telephone) was used to subsidize another (for example, mail). The value of the service to any buyer was enhanced if others also had it. As examples, a telephone is more useful if everybody has telephones connected to the same network or the individual's protection against a plague improves when adequate health care is universally available.

Even regulated producers could gain from tight regulation: reduced competition and legal collusion on rate setting guaranteed prof-itability. Those firms that could not retain monopoly profits derived from regulatory protection might still prefer regulation. For example, buying peace with labor is sometimes easier if the financial gains from government-restricted competition (for example, in the airlines) can be partly dedicated to paying workers higher wages.[26]

Today, however, several factors advance greater competition in the provision of services. First, merit services are almost universally provided in most industrial countries. The average user will not gain much if universal service is extended to those few without it. Indeed, most users would not be seriously hurt by a modest rollback in service coverage, for example, if higher prices in the aftermath of deregula-tion forced 1 percent of U.S. households to lose their phone service. Second, the recent experience with high inflation weakens support for regulation because it gives consumers, especially large commercial users, a stronger incentive to question the advantage of exchanging reliability for price. Third, advances in technology have increased the importance of the price and the availability of hardware capable of providing new service options. This increased importance, in turn, prompts business users to demand more service options on more competitive terms. It also gives potential entrants into the hardware supply or product service fields tremendous incentives to push for more competition. Most of the battle against AT&T's domination of the phone industry was carried on for years by small hardware firms that could make large profits by taking over small pieces of the AT&T equipment market. (This was the case in the 1968 *Carterfone* decision.) Similarly, today regional airline carriers are an important voice in opposing any move to reregulate airlines in the United States.

The same forces are at work outside the United States. Deregula-tion would provide an opportunity to consider international rational-ization of services through lowering barriers to trade in services. Nonetheless, progress domestically and internationally will be slow and painful. Protected monopolies, such as the Postal Telegraph and Telecommunication administrations, will likely oppose actions that would diminish their power. They may even adopt "white elephant strategies" to make it extremely expensive for users or the government to dismantle their authority and monopoly power.[27] Nevertheless, the trends in domestic regulation apparently may slowly permit consider-ation of freer trade in services.

Even with minimal deregulation and privatization elsewhere, however, freer trade in services might be developed. This develop-ment would depend on finding a way to ensure fair, economic compe-tition between private firms and government monopolies. A precedent exists under GATT article 17, which provides that the state trading-enterprises shall make their purchases and sales "solely in accordance with commercial considerations." The article also provides that "foreign competitors will be given an adequate opportunity to compete for participation in such purchases or sales" and requires that state trading-enterprises "act in a manner consistent with the general principles of nondiscriminatory treatment."

At present article 17 applies partly to services insofar as their trade is complementary to trade in goods. When conceived the article was meant "to be limited to products as understood in commercial practice, and not intended to include the purchase or sale of services." It is now desirable, however, to extend this principle to services. The *U.S. National Study on Trade in Services* suggests that

> state service enterprises could be required to follow nondiscriminatory procedures in providing those services necessary for foreign service importers to compete with domestic companies, to purchase services based, to the extent possible, on quality, price and other commercial factors regardless of whether those services were supplied by domestic or foreign concerns. In addition, the obligation for state service monopolies to compete with foreign and domestic concerns on an arms-length commercial basis might be identified as a longer-term objective for inclusion under this article. Exceptions, of course, would have to be developed and specified to account for legitimate national interests.[28]

Article 17 does not apply to government purchases from state firms. Therefore, some extension of GATT's Government Procurement Code to services is desirable.

Without some version of article 17, the potential for serious service trade disputes may increase. The United States expressed serious concern when in mid-1982 Nordic and Benelux Postal, Telegraph, and Telephone (PTT) administrations sought to limit the number of U.S. suppliers of new information services between their countries and the United States. After months of delay, the PTTs backed down, but they did not admit that their requests were in any way misdirected.[29] In addition, U.S. firms worry that a foreign PTT or firm could receive a license to conduct international business between the United States and its home country without granting reciprocal entry and benefits to U.S. firms. If this situation occurred, all the traffic flowing between the home country and the United States could be channeled to the foreign subsidiary, thereby putting the U.S. firms at a serious competitive disadvantage.[30]

In summary, the evolution of the world economy is making many of the standard reasons for maintaining regulated economies obsolete. Continuation of traditional regulatory and competitive policies outside the United States may ease because of domestic considerations, not because of U.S. pressure. The easing of such policies would provide great opportunity for establishing freer trade in services. Even if entrenched monopolies and bureaucracies do not allow or initiate privatization and deregulation, however, countries could develop new principles to permit the competitive sale of services across national borders within the GATT framework. This solution to the service issue would be minimal. In the next section we examine GATT as a guide to more thorough reform.

Applying GATT to Trade in Services

GATT dealt with trade in goods, not trade in services. Its main focus was on reducing barriers to trade imposed at borders. More generally, it tried to persuade countries to reduce discriminatory treatment that favored domestic products over foreign imports. GATT provides not for free trade of goods but rather for a framework and mechanism to allow countries to progress toward freer trade. The contracting parties, to make GATT viable, excluded some products from its reach, granted some exceptions to most-favored-nation treatment, and provided escape routes and safety nets to allow countries suffering severe short-term problems to escape temporarily from their obligations. At the same time, GATT does provide for specific mechanisms to settle disputes and to minimize prolonged cheating.

There is general agreement that extending GATT directly to services is impractical. Many of the rules, principles, and procedures embodied in GATT, however, are relevant to services. If countries choose to establish trade rules for services, it will be easier to start with what exists in GATT than to start from scratch. (New rules or organizations could be contemplated to build on what is borrowed from GATT or if negotiations within GATT lead nowhere.) Further, two structural elements embodied in GATT make it superior to the OECD as a trade forum: "(1) it is contractually binding and (2) it applies to a large number of developed and developing countries."[31] In contrast, the OECD has only twenty-four developed countries and works on a consensus basis. Its ability to impose its decisions on deviating members is severely limited.

Certain GATT articles and codes are critical to any attempt to modify GATT to cover services. Some sense of the problems that lay before negotiators can be garnered by examining key GATT articles and codes and projecting their possible applicability to services.

24

Most-Favored-Nation Treatment. Progress toward free trade in goods under GATT occurred because GATT rules subtly increased the size of potential gains from trade while deterring practices that hampered free trade. GATT article 1, which calls for most-favored-nation (MFN) treatment among contracting parties, was particularly important in encouraging universal, multilateral liberalization. Concessions to one trading partner have to be provided to all GATT contracting parties on an equivalent basis. (This idea remains central to GATT even though it has eroded under the demands by developing countries for generalized preferences in their trading relations with industrial countries.) Countries could decide to what degree they would open their markets to trade, but they could not discriminate among trading partners when granting concessions. In addition, because GATT used the same principle to govern all trade in goods, industries seeking exceptions in the GATT system had to prove their case. GATT continually sought universal bargains among its contracting parties to prevent discriminatory trade practices.

Application of the MFN concept to services would probably be on a conditional basis. This means that any commitments about trade in services would be extended only to participating countries that accepted a common framework of principles, rules, and procedures. Some modifications of traditional MFN practices are likely to be needed, however. Where it makes economic sense to limit the number of firms providing a service, rules for allocating opportunities among a limited number of foreign and domestic concerns will be necessary. Further, when some countries or groups of countries undertake greater levels of obligation in trading among themselves, some mechanism analogous to the free trade areas permitted under GATT may need to be devised for services. Finally, exceptions to MFN treatment for developing countries analogous to the preferences they now receive might be negotiated for services. Developing countries would, in effect, be allowed to postpone implementation of new rules.

National Treatment. GATT article 3 requires that imported goods receive treatment equivalent to domestically produced merchandise once barriers at the border have been cleared. It provides that products "be accorded treatment no less favorable than that accorded to like products of national origin in respect to all laws, regulations and requirements affecting their internal sale, purchase, transportation, distribution, or use." Internal regulation of services in most countries exceeds regulation on goods. Although article 3 does not apply to services, a prime goal would be to establish national treatment disciplines covering services. The strict application of article 3, however,

25

may benefit established domestic firms and favor foreign firms already established to the prejudice of potential entrants. For example, a country can allow foreign banks to establish local branches but then forbid them from providing the most important individual services. Restrictions on foreign exchange transactions may be much more onerous to foreign banks than to domestic ones that conduct little international business. Again, a restriction that prevents all entry into a new service may strictly live up to national treatment standards while actually favoring those firms already established in a market.

Trade in Services versus Investment in Services. Traditionally governments have tried to separate trade and investment issues. In general, trade disciplines have been more comprehensive than those for investment. Yet many countries contend that investment is required to sell services internationally. Therefore, they argue, trade in services *is* an investment issue. No effort to apply GATT disciplines to services can succeed unless countries are convinced that trade rules for services are possible without becoming entangled with touchy issues of investment in services.

Countries have to distinguish between trade and investment in a service, between the component of the service that is traded (that is, produced abroad) and the component of the service that requires investment and local production. In some instances this distinction is relatively clear. For example, data processing provided from a foreign center via long-distance communication links is trade. The same service provided within a country by a foreign-owned computer-processing service is an investment activity. At other times the distinction is clouded. Moreover, some countries demand that foreign entities establish operations in their border as a condition for doing business (for example, in insurance). Under this circumstance, investment requirements become a trade issue.

Ultimately, the critical distinction is not between trade and investment but between the right of establishment and the right to do business. Establishment issues in their pure form are likely to remain outside GATT's competence. As long as foreign services that have overcome barriers to entry into the market are granted equitable access to the distribution system, however, they may be able to compete with domestic service suppliers.

The existing GATT approach to the distribution system could be applied to trade in services. Thus, access to a local distribution system would be treated as a trade issue, while ownership of the distribution system would be treated as an investment issue. Access to the distribution system would

26

include the right of a foreign supplier of services to negotiate a contract with local businesses to provide distribution or servicing facilities. Thus, for example, if the national treatment principle were adopted for trade in services, a foreign insurance company that was able to overcome the agreed restrictions at the border would have a right to sign a contract with local insurance brokers or claims adjusters to sell their policies and handle the claims.[32]

Barriers at the Border. The areas for which GATT provides the sketchiest roadmap for services are customs valuation, location of barriers, the relevance of subsidies and quantitative restrictions, and the provision of appropriate remedies through agreed-upon dispute settlement mechanisms. Goods are easier to count and value than services. GATT provides that when barriers to trade on goods are imposed they should be done so at the border. Critics contend that the GATT system has had so much trouble coping with protectionist pressures on goods that it is illusory to expect progress on the more difficult problem of services.

Indeed, many obstacles to trade in services are not imposed at the border. It is not clear how the value of services could be computed for customs. In addition, the identification and computation of subsidies for services is much more difficult than for goods. (Most service subsidies are domestic in nature; they are harder to deal with than export subsidies.) Quantitative restrictions also seem to have less likelihood of succeeding for services than for goods. It is doubtful, in fact, that any mechanism for computing the level of distortion as contained in the antidumping code could be devised for services. The nature of obstacles that restrict trade in services often appear less overtly protectionist in nature than many barriers to trade in goods. An aggrieved party has more difficulty proving that obstacles were meant to be restrictive and were not simply legitimate national efforts to ensure national cultural, political, and security interests. In short, these are the areas in which the current GATT articles and codes are least directly applicable to services. Much more thinking will be required to deal with these problems.

Procedures: Transparency, Notification, and Dispute Settlement. Many of the procedures of GATT might be extended to services. They may not be as easily administered when applied to services instead of goods, however. For instance, the concept that obstacles to trade should be transparent and that countries would notify their barriers as a step toward allowing negotiations is more difficult for services for

27

which the barriers are not at the border and the line between legitimate and protectionist barriers is indistinct. Similarly, for the reasons cited above, it may be difficult to apply current dispute settlement procedures directly to services. The idea that a dispute settlement procedure with some enforcement capacity should exist is as applicable to services as to goods, but the details of the process may have to be modified extensively.

GATT MTN Codes. GATT is not and was not meant to be a static institution. During the Multilateral Trade Negotiations (MTN) in the 1970s, codes applicable to nontariff barriers were negotiated. Although these codes have only limited direct application to services traded in conjunction with goods, they contain considerable promise for trade in services. Three codes seem particularly promising.

The Agreement on Government Procurement explicitly requires signatories to consider its extension to services. In November 1983 negotiations began to broaden and improve this code's application. Signatories are currently required not to discriminate against or among the products of other signatories in purchases covered by the agreement. It contains detailed requirements about how government purchases are to be conducted, and, to ensure compliance, the code details explicit mechanisms for dispute settlement. The United States has tried, so far without success, to persuade other signatories to interpret the agreement to cover leasing contracts that could circumvent the code. The possibilities of applying this code to services remain.

The Standards Code, more formally called the Agreement on Technical Barriers to Trade, requires that signatories adopt standards and technical regulations, engage in testing, and conduct certification procedures in ways that do not unnecessarily obstruct trade. The standards code applies to all agricultural and industrial products but not to services. Extending the Standards Code, however, might be realistic and extremely useful for such services as telecommunications in which design, testing, and performance standards prevent foreign firms from competing with or even interconnecting with domestic networks. To agree upon standards for services, of course, may be more difficult than to do so for goods.

The Customs Valuation Code provides detailed rules for the determination of the customs value of dutiable goods. This code applies to service to some extent because it also prescribes whether or not certain associated services are to form part of the dutiable value of importer merchandise. Extending this code to services that are traded independent of goods would involve major difficulties, however. It may be possible to extend and modify the code to limit the abuse of valuation procedures that unnecessarily inflate the service component of a good. Although some analysts in and out of government disagree, we believe it will be very difficult to extend the already weak Subsidies Code to services in any comprehensive form.

All in all, there seem to be major opportunities for extending existing GATT articles and codes to services, but doing so will not be possible without considerable work and creativity. Some of the special problems that must be overcome to make GATT a useful forum in which to treat services are considered in the next chapter.

4

Special Problems for Services Negotiations

Chapter 2 suggested that most countries could eventually profit from freer trade in services. Governments, however, are natural skeptics. A proven potential for gain does not automatically attract their support. Governments worry as much about how to avoid sharp temporary losses as they do about the potential for gains. Therefore, before a free trade system is likely to be enacted, it must promise to raise expected benefits and reduce the chances of serious temporary losses simultaneously.

The struggle to establish free trade in goods after World War II profited from the linking of three factors. First, the United States dominated the world economy and was the political superpower. The United States chose to use its strength to support free trade. Second, the long, sustained world economic expansion made it easier for countries to move from rhetorical to actual support of free trade in the negotiations during the 1950s and 1960s. As long as the economic pie was growing, cooperation on achieving freer trade was simplified. Third, the economic attributes of commodities and manufactured goods made it relatively easy to define workable trade rules and monitor their compliance.

Efforts to liberalize trade in services face more significant obstacles. The diffusion of international economic and political power in the last three decades, the uneven performance of the world economy in recent years, and the unique characteristics of traded services together create special problems. First, they make it hard to show that a general agreement on services has a high discounted present value for most countries. Second, they make the task of monitoring and enforcing bargains more difficult. Third, they weaken the safety net that has cushioned countries from some consequences of accepting freer trade. This chapter spells out these difficulties and their implications in greater detail.

Discounted Present Value

The current benefit of freer trade in services equals the benefit from this particular year plus the discounted present value of future benefits. (The present value equals the amount of money earned today that would equal future earnings if multiplied by the appropriate annual interest rate. For example, one dollar today is worth $1.10 next year at a 10 percent annual interest rate. The discounted value is the present value of future earnings after allowing for the possibility that one may not earn the future revenue at all. If there is only a 50 percent chance of being paid, the discounted value of a one dollar debt is fifty cents.) If nations calculate in terms of discounted present value, two items become crucial for judging the merits of free trade—whether a country expects benefits or costs in future years and over how many years do they expect the benefits or costs to endure?

If a country expects a competitive success under free trade eventually, will it accept immediate losses (perhaps fairly large ones) to promote freer trade? If a country has a high degree of confidence that free trade will persist for many years, it can afford to tolerate initial losses in return for later gains.[33] The reason is straightforward: a long period of expected benefits cancels out immediate losses under discounted present value.

After 1945 the United States was the dominant economic and political power, and it clearly benefited from free trade. It did not take much imagination for other countries to guess that the United States would commit its formidable resources to ensuring freer trade. Therefore, other countries assumed a higher probability of a long period of free trade.

If U.S. dominance heightened confidence in the durability of free trade, it did not automatically determine the calculation of whether a country would generally profit or lose from trade. Another factor, however—the longest continuous economic boom in history—made the potential pain of free competition more palatable. A country could expect to export more as world trade grew even if its share of the world market shrank.

Events in recent years have made the cost-benefit calculus of free trade shakier. The erosion of U.S. power has undercut confidence in free trade because it depends on the political support of several major powers rather than on the urgings of one.[34] Also, the uneven record of the world economy since 1970 and the stagnant trade performance since 1981 have forced many readjustments. Such developments do not build confidence in the prospects of growing markets and positive returns from competition under free trade. Both adverse developments for free trade are more serious for services than for goods. The practice of free trade in goods is well established.[35] Services do not enjoy this advantage.

Presidential pronouncements extolling renewed U.S. strength notwithstanding, little can be done about the underlying shifts in global economic power. Therefore, one can expect different opportunities for liberalization depending on whether or not a sector tends toward highly cyclical performance, uncertain prospects for long-term growth, and extended periods of surplus productive capacity. Services fitting these criteria are poorer prospects for liberalization. U.S. officials should not allow their special problems to ruin a negotiation on services. For example, negotiators should make telecommunication and accounting far more important than shipping. Traditional lines of insurance are less promising than other financial services, and construction has less promise than specialized design services.

While no single factor can be a good predictor of the chances for free trade, it is useful to ask what negotiators could do about services with greatly varying returns in terms of discounted present value. In particular, should they try to maintain the principle of universal rules and standards, or should they acknowledge the differences among services? In the closing pages of this paper we suggest some guidelines.

Monitoring and Enforcement

Even if the prospects are otherwise promising for free trade, nations try to make sure that others are not cheating and taking advantage of them. With limited exceptions, countries want to ensure reciprocity. When honored, reciprocity guarantees that by opening its markets to others a country will gain new markets for its own exports.

Regrettably, pledges of good faith concerning reciprocity are insufficient guarantees for most governments. They require some practical power to monitor compliance and retaliate at acceptable costs. Early in the history of GATT, the United States' power in the world allowed it to be an informal policeman if it so chose. All countries wanted access to the U.S. market, and the United States could force reciprocity if it so desired. (Sometimes, however, the United States considered reciprocity less important than other objectives.)[36] If trade diplomacy proved inadequate, the United States could use its leverage on other issues to nudge the offender. Even if compliance was imperfect, U.S. power sufficed to make reciprocity credible.

Even after U.S. power peaked, the credibility of reciprocity was high.[37] The largest share of world exports remained in the hands of relatively few nations, each of which had a clear stake in encouraging trade. In this sense the world trade system had a structure similar to that of an industrial oligopoly. Each "firm" (for example, France) had a large enough share of the market to cooperate with its rival to avoid ruinous forms of competition. As long as only a few nations controlled the bulk of trade, it was easier to coordinate trade negotiations and to spend the time and resources necessary to make side payments to sweeten the terms for trade concessions.

Irrespective of the concentration of power, trading in goods presented an easier enforcement problem than trade in services presents. The critical barriers to the trade in goods were usually located at the border. Tariffs and quotas, and later various nontariff barriers at the border, were the bane of free trade; but at least they were relatively transparent, and therefore retaliation against cheaters was reasonable. GATT rules permitted a certain tidiness to the process that further enhanced stability. In essence, these rules allowed countries to retaliate in precise ways and encouraged considerable pauses for negotiations and second thoughts.

Commerce in some services raises a problem with cheating that GATT cannot easily address. When right of entry into a service market is limited by restricting the firms allowed to do business locally, problems arise. Such restrictions can be subtle, difficult to identify, and hard to prove as protectionist. Further, it is extremely difficult to measure the effect of such measures, and therefore they are hard to bargain about in an unconditional, multilateral framework. Other governments find it difficult to detect and prove that barriers to services are primarily meant to be protectionist. Many of the barriers are based on legitimate cultural, social, and security concerns and are genuinely not meant to be protectionist, but protectionism may be an unintended consequence. Even if protectionism is possible to prove, it is difficult to imagine how to phrase unconditional multilateral concessions to encourage reciprocity. Unlike tariffs and quotas, a barrier in one domestic market may not be a barrier in another market, and the array of potential barriers is bewildering.

In light of the difficulties just cited, any plan for negotiations on services will be difficult to devise. More fundamentally, the plan may have to depart from the principles of multilateral reciprocity on an unconditional basis that we described in our application of GATT principles to services. In the close of this paper we discuss when such departures from the traditional approach are necessary. In particular we seek to establish methods to take advantage of bilateral conditional reciprocity to organize services where cheating is endemic.

33

Safety Nets

The discussion of U.S power, prolonged prosperity, and cheating has so far neglected a strategic choice taken after 1945 that greatly enhanced the chances of achieving free trade. All three of the factors so far analyzed pertained to making countries believe that long periods of prosperous free trading were credible and therefore that temporary losses were acceptable. The United States, under prodding from Britain, however, also accepted a commitment to limit at any given time the degree of losses from free trade and investment. To an extent unrivaled in earlier eras of free trade, the Bretton Woods system rested on systematic, international public guarantees of assistance to ease the rigors associated with international competition for individual countries.[38]

After World War II the United States committed its financial resources and access to its markets, often on a nonreciprocal basis, to important nations that suffered because of the transition toward free trade. In addition, the trade rules recognized such devices as temporary escape clauses to ease industrial adjustment problems. The IMF and the World Bank had the power to provide limited financial assistance to reduce the pain of liberalization. Altogether these measures made the worst risks of free trade less acute. They also, however, threatened to discourage adjustment to competitive realities and to mask protectionism if countries decided to abuse them. Luckily, continuing prosperity largely removed the incentives for such behavior until recently, especially because the international assistance was not lucrative enough to match the benefits of successful trade expansion.

The downturn in the world economy since the early 1970s removed the certainty of an expanding pie and strained the adequacy of the safety net. This situation has prompted the creation of many temporary relief mechanisms that limit competition, such as voluntary limits on exports to troubled markets. The risk for service liberalization is that the new strands of the safety net will hamper efforts to free trade in services.

Trade negotiators concerned with services must find ways to limit the size of losses for a given country without endorsing undue trade restrictions. For the poorer countries some form of new financial assistance is logical. But the richer countries have to decide if universal trade rules are the best route to controlling risks. One alternative is to encourage groups of countries into trading blocks for services. While such a maneuver brings back dark memories of the autarkic practices of the 1930s, it also could establish a series of building blocks for future global integration of the industry. Regional groups may be at odds with the idea of treating different industries according to their own functional logic, however. Which approach should dominate the service talks?

New Directions for Trade in Services

Chapter 4 has so far argued that three problems will create a predictable pattern of exceptions to GATT-style free trade in services. The sharply varying prospects for growth in different service industries will make it difficult to liberalize some parts of the service sector. The difficulties of monitoring and enforcing the rules under current conditions for some services make a form of strict reciprocity in granting trade concessions more attractive. And the tattered safety net for services could lead to experimentation with specialized subgroups of like-minded countries to organize some parts of the service trade. This section suggests some tentative guidelines to reconcile these developments with the creation of more universal principles and negotiations concerning the service trade.

As negotiators confront the problems pertaining to services, it is useful to recall that strategic commodities, agricultural products, and some sensitive manufacturing industries have long deviated from the GATT ideal.[39] The key to managing these individual conflicts from the viewpoint of the overall trade system has been a combination of two tactics. Either countries have tacitly acknowledged that a few extraordinarily sensitive items are subject only to imperfect applications of the rules (as in agriculture or oil), or they have demanded a substitute for trade liberalization, namely investment opportunities. For example, countries considered automobiles to be a vital component of an industrial economy. As a result, they insisted on a successful long-term presence in the industry (either as a general manufacturer or specialized supplier). The pressing question for trade was how to reconcile this claim with the spirit of GATT. The answer was a de facto bargain that countries had to provide effective access to their market if others strongly demanded it through either trade or investment.[40] A format for organizing the services trade should make similar bargains possible.

Some element of universalism requires that general codes for all the services be established by multilateral negotiations. Yet these codes have to acknowledge the tendencies so far outlined. In addition to laying out the general principles described earlier in chapter 3, we believe that future agreements might feature four special arrangements: (1) a negotiated definition of the specific segments of all of the services industries; (2) a fast track tariff that would be scheduled for phase-out in advance; (3) a series of provisos that govern all other international agreements concerning individual segments of the service trade (or regional trading agreements about all services); and (4) an agreement on which segments may be organized according to the principle of bilateral reciprocity. Together these arrangements would minimize the aggregate protectionist effect of the deviations from universal liberal principles. If countries also added special assistance to developing countries to bolster their position in services, the makings of a new regime for services would be in place.

Everyone recognizes that some parts of the service trade are particularly difficult to bring under a system of free trade. The U.S. National Services study, for example, acknowledges that the United Nations Conference on Trade and Development (UNCTAD) liner code is likely to remove most of shipping from the purview of free trade. Finance ministries and central banks are not likely to relinquish their grasp over monetary policy to accommodate free trade advocates.[41] But in most industries only selected segments of the trade are out of reach of liberalization. For example, developing countries often restrict sales of car and life insurance, which are easy to supply on a local basis, but they may accept other forms of foreign-supplied insurance.

A good set of trade rules can sharpen the distinctions among the market segments so that regulations about one do not spill over into another. A simple way is to establish a common international classification for the purposes of trade of all of the market segments. Besides encouraging more selective treatments of markets, the exercise would have the salutary effect of teaching countries about the extent of intra-industry specialization in trade. As we noted earlier, such specialization has made trade in goods far more palatable for nations. At present they seem not to recognize comparable distinctions about services.

In addition to defining segments, countries should also have to signify barriers to trade in those specified services. Moreover they ought to be obliged to convert acknowledged barriers into tariffs to the maximum extent possible. R. E. Baldwin and T. S. Thompson have an idea of special merit in this regard. They urge the creation of a fast track system of review that would permit injured nations to raise their tariffs quickly and repeatedly until effective protection was achieved. This system would discourage quotas and nontariff barriers. As a price for the fast track the country would have to establish a schedule for the tariff's elimination.[42]

The process of classification and notification would begin to draw distinctions between what services are and are not covered and between what obstacles are and are not protectionist. Once these distinctions are made, another rule could stipulate that each signatory nation must respond to inquiries about which national regulations cover what segment of the market according to the official definitions. This rule would stop a good deal of obstruction by indirect regulation. (An official definition of segments would also simplify trade problems concerning bilateral reciprocity.)

Other international agreements concerning service markets pose an even more fundamental problem for universal GATT rules. The rules of the International Telecommunication Union, the UNCTAD liner code, and the International Civil Aviation Organization agreements all organize individual service markets according to universal international agreements. In many cases they do, or someday may, run counter to liberal trade rules. Yet there is a clear and pressing need for more detailed expert agreements to deal with the special properties of some markets, and there will be great political pressure for some special arrangements for particular markets.

Sovereign nations have the right to be inconsistent, so little is to be done in any strictly constitutional sense about divergent international agreements. The United States, however, could advocate principles to govern other international agreements—in essence, a protocol on how to reconcile GATT with other sets of rules. Ideally this protocol would establish an obligation on the part of the new services signatories to negotiate other agreements in good faith to fit the GATT framework. In the process, some modification of current GATT rules might be negotiated. For its part GATT must evolve to accommodate the changing international trading situation. Trade restrictions under other agreements that deviate from GATT rules could be challenged under the GATT grievance machinery.

Such a protocol has a special advantage in regard to new international agreements. If regional groupings or the OECD nations pursue selective liberalization that goes beyond the global standards, it would limit their options to methods that are compatible with GATT. In particular, there should be an understanding that any agreement among these like-minded states be open to other GATT members.[43] This understanding should provide some safeguards for the developing countries. In the case of regional experiments by developing countries, the emphasis should be somewhat different. Because these experiments represent a much smaller share of the market and of world power, the danger is not so much unfair trade as a complete abnegation of liberal principles. The correct point for negotiations may be uniform treatment for investment or the right to do business by third parties. In the cases of both rich and poor countries the overall goal should be the same: to allow selective experimentation by some countries to become a building block for later liberalization by others.

As we argued earlier, in the early stages of greater trade competition it may be possible to establish safety nets more easily within regional or selected bilateral agreements than through universal accords. A universal framework for fostering trade must allow for some experimentation with appropriate sizing of cooperative groups of nations when dealing with new terrain.[44]

Finally, the problems of enforcement and monitoring, plus sensitivity about national security in some cases, lead many to advocate strict bilateral reciprocity as the key to expanding trade in services. This approach stresses strict equivalent concessions on the right to compete in services on a bilateral basis. Reciprocity allows the United States to use its best weapon, access of other countries' firms to the U.S. market, to exact precisely the same privileges for its companies.

Recent work in bargaining and game theory indicate that approaches akin to strict reciprocity can lead to more general and enduring forms of cooperation. This cooperation occurs so long as each contending party adopts a "tit-for-tat" strategy so that it matches cooperation with cooperation (and retaliation with retaliation). In this case the United States would announce its willingness to grant liberal reciprocal concessions. Whenever a country matched it, so much the better. If a country later reneged, so would the United States until that country mended its ways.

The experiments in game theory are also subject to some problems that suggest caution in their application. In particular, when many parties are acting simultaneously, it is hard to judge when, who, and how each party is acting. Nuanced reciprocity in timely direct response to the other countries' actions may be very difficult to achieve. Moreover, the costs of making such bargains work when there are several players in extremely dynamic markets are likely to be high.[45] There is a serious chance of misperception that could lead to escalating trade conflicts.

Given the limitations of reciprocity, reserving it for especially tendentious markets is wise. International negotiations could establish a category of industry segments authorized to experiment with bilateral reciprocity. The logical candidates would be those with the weakest prospects for liberalization. Such an approach has the double advantage of putting enormous pressure on countries to be selective in choosing the markets and limiting fears about an endless escalation of such practices.

Together the practices of stricter definition of industry segments, a fast track tariff, a protocol on the relation between GATT and other international agreements, more assistance for developing countries in the services sector, and an official designation of acceptable markets for reciprocity arrangements would ease many of the problems outlined in this paper. These practices allow flexibility about what would be liberalized without fanning fears that protectionism will endlessly escalate. They permit countries to experiment with freer trade in ways that limit the worst risks of loss. And they allow the tough discipline of bilateral reciprocity to be applied to segments of the market where multilateralism might be only a fig leaf on widespread cheating in the marketplace.

Notes

1. A typical vague definition of services appears in "Liberalization of Trade in Services," a United Kingdom private sector assessment paper prepared by the Liberalisation of Trade in Services Committee of the Committee on Invisible Exports, November 1982, p. 16. LOTIS states that service industries "constitute those activities which provide a service in contrast to goods which supply goods."

2. Even if unanimous agreement about what activities to include as services existed, serious data problems would persist because data collection systems were designed with goods in mind and it is easier to count and value goods than services. Balance-of-payments accounts do not pick up sales abroad by foreign affiliates, customs documents on individual transactions exist for traded goods but not for services, and services are often provided in a package jointly with goods. Moreover, it is harder to know how an inventory of services will accrue or depreciate in value; and the domestic underground economy, which is made up mostly of services, is notoriously difficult to measure. "The Underground Economy's Hidden Force," *Business Week* (April 5, 1982), pp. 64–70.

3. From 1948 to mid-1983 the number of U.S. workers producing manufactured goods rose from 15.6 million to 18.6 million. Employment in services tripled from 20.9 million to 66.2 million workers. Thus about fifteen new service jobs were created for each new manufacturing job. Also between 1950 and 1980 the percentage of U.S. manufacturing workers engaged in production jobs fell from 82 percent to 70 percent. While there were about 3.8 million new jobs in manufacturing employment created between 1948 and 1978, only about one-sixth were in production jobs. Many of the rest were service workers. Eli Ginzberg and George Vojta, "The Service Sector in the U.S. Economy," *Scientific American*, vol. 244, no. 3 (March 1981); U.S. Government, *U.S. National Study on Trade in Services* (A Report to GATT) (December 1983), section 2.A (hereafter cited as *U.S. National Study*).

4. In 1972 about 15 percent of manufacturing firms' outside purchases went for services, and the figure is steadily increasing. About one-fourth of U.S. GNP consists of services used as input by goods-producing industries. U.S. Government, *U.S. National Study,* section 2.A.

5. Charles Jonscher, "Information Resources and Economic Productivity," *Information Economics and Policy*, vol. 1 (1983), pp. 13–35. See also, "A Productivity Revolution in the Service Sector," *Business Week* (September 5, 1983), p. 106.

6. The distinction between trade and investment in measures is conceptually clear but very difficult to measure in existing data. This distinction turns out to be quite important politically because international rules and institu-

tions dealing with trade and investment are separate. Thus it is easier to argue that the GATT should be extended to cover trade in services than to cover investment in services. See the discussion of this distinction in *U.S. National Study* and in Robert A. Feldman and Allen J. Proctor, "U.S. International Trade in Services," *Federal Reserve Bank of New York Review* (Spring 1983), pp. 30–36.

7. *U.S. National Study*, appendix 1, table 1.

8. U.S. Trade Representative calculations from IMF balance-of-payments statistics. The estimates here are revisions of data presented in the *U.S. National Study*. Figures that use $35 billion as 1980 U.S. service exports are derived from the study itself and also those used in the Economic Consulting Services study.

9. As noted above, the data reveal that only 28.8 percent of recorded U.S. service exports in 1980 came from the more dynamic "other private services." This figure was tenth of the top twelve service exporters, followed only by Japan (27.1 percent) and Spain (13.8 percent). When compared to the top developing country service exporters, the United States trails South Korea (51.7 percent), Singapore (32.3 percent), Yugoslavia (32.2 percent), but leads Mexico (32.3 percent), Egypt (19.0 percent), and Saudi Arabia (17.2 percent). It is interesting that Canada which has tried to promote exports of sophisticated services derived a healthy 37.8 percent of its exports from the "other" category and that the laggards were in fact developed countries, Norway (14.9 percent) and Australia (8.1 percent). The pattern is thus quite mixed and can be expected to stay that way. On one hand, the U.S. share of banking and construction/engineering dominance has eroded. On the other hand, U.S. advertising firms remain dominant on international exports of advertising services. *U.S. National Study*, appendix 1, table 3, p. 114.

10. Economic Consulting Services, *The International Operations of U.S. Service Industries: Current Data Collection and Analysis* (Prepared for the U.S. Departments of State and Commerce and the Office of the U.S. Trade Representative) (June 1981).

11. Ibid., pp. 242, 264, 267.

12. We made this rough calculation because ECS, *International Operations*, apparently identified half of U.S. investment receipts as service exports.

13. An analogy from the world automobile industry will clarify this point. An examination of automobile trade figures would not accurately reflect the degree to which automobiles are produced and sold by other than local national firms. The reason, of course, is that most American automobile sales in the vast European market are accounted for through the production and sales of European subsidiaries. Automobile trade figures show only the small percentage of total revenues repatriated to American parents (or the flow of its parts to and from national subsidiaries). Similarly, many of the foreign service revenues of American firms are generated by subsidiaries and local offices located abroad.

14. Oliver E. Williamson, *Markets and Hierarchies* (New York: Free Press, 1975). David McClain, "Foreign Direct Investment in the United States: Old Currents, 'New Waves,' and the Theory of Direct Investment" in Charles P.

Kindelberger and David Audretsch, eds., *The Multinational Corporation in the 1980s* (Cambridge: M.I.T. Press, 1983), pp. 278–333.

15. Charles R. Morris, *Los Angeles Times* (January 1, 1984), part 4, p. 2. A fuller sample of the history of the U.S. government and its international banks would include Stuart Robinson, *Multinational Banking* (Leiden: A. W. Sitjhoff, 1972); Fred Block, *The Origins of International Economic Disorder* (Berkeley: University of California, 1977); Jonathan David Aronson, *Money and Power* (Beverly Hills: Sage, 1977).

16. Stephen Clarkson, *Canada and the Reagan Challenge* (Toronto: James Lorimer and Co., 1982), pp. 236–37. This work was sponsored by the Canadian Institute for Economic Policy.

17. A paean to the growth of financial services briefly dismisses most of the worries reflected in this line of reasoning. "The New York Colossus," *Business Week* (July 23, 1984), pp. 98–112.

The argument about British decline is best stated in Susan Strange, *Sterling and British Policy* (New York: Oxford, 1971). Robert Gilpin was one of the first to note the parallel to the United States when he questioned the policies favoring overseas direct investment in his book, *U.S. Power and the Multinational Corporation* (New York: Basic Books, 1975). The questioning of the new role of services, especially financial services, in U.S. economic and trade policy is explored in unpublished work by Stephen Cohen and John Zysman as well as Peter Gourevitch. We thank them for showing us their book manuscripts.

18. Based on interviews at the OECD in 1982 and 1983.

19. The U.S. would be competitive in some smokestack service industries even after international liberalization. The United States can still prosper in those services where it has a vast pool of skilled workers and good technical facilities remain in place. When Britain lost its competitive advantages in many manufacturing industries in the nineteenth century, the British remained highly competitive in manufacturing ventures that required medium-sized plants and many skilled workers for precision manufacturing. (It faded in industries requiring large new plants and new mixes of corporate finance, organization and technical personnel.) The United States surely has some enduring advantages in traditional services.

20. The combination of shorter product lives, more specialized products, and growing importance of global production and distribution strategies, when combined with lower costs and greater sophistication in production make for very complicated managerial problems. Firms experience more difficult problems concerning the internal and external coordination of their operations. Therefore, the demand for specialized services to coordinate production and distribution is growing. Although some of these services are traditionally performed by headquarters groups, the demand for many of these services is too sporadic to justify the establishment of large, full-time units within the corporation. When there are many large companies, all of which have intermittent demand for specialized services, third-party companies to provide assistance in production and distribution tasks will become a major part of the service economy. As companies become truly multinational

in their outlook and division of labor, so too becomes the supporting network of service providers. Thomas M. Stanback, Jr., et al., *Services in the New Economy* (Totowa, New Jersey: Allanheld, Osmun & Co., 1981).

Andre Sapir has conducted valuable studies along these lines that he summarizes in "Trade in Services: Policy Issues for the Eighties," *Columbia Journal of World Business* (Fall 1982), pp. 77–82. Sapir argues that the principles of comparative advantage and economies of scale apply to services and that trade advantages in goods and services are complementary. See also, Alan V. Deardorff, "Comparative Advantage and International Trade and Investment in Services," paper presented at the 3rd Annual Workshop on U.S.-Canadian Relations (Current Issues in Trade and Investment in Service Industries: U.S.-Canadian Bilateral and Multilateral Perspectives), Ann Arbor, Michigan, October 19, 1984.

21. Paul Krugman, "New Theories of Trade among Industrial Countries," *American Economic Review*, vol. 73, no. 21 (May 1983), pp. 343–46.

22. "Community Shifts Stand on Trade in Services," *Financial Times* (October 19, 1983).

23. "GATT Consensus May Soon Emerge on Code for Trade in Services," *Financial Times* (October 24, 1983).

24. Authors' conversation with official in the Office of the U.S. Trade Representative, December 15, 1983, and with Latin American officials on May 30, 1984.

25. Even large business users often favor this formula because of the difficulty of making inventories of many services. Therefore, business users willingly paid a premium for reliability as long as the alternative supply systems are few. When changes in technology, finance, or the scale of the market make competing possible for numerous alternative suppliers, however, the incentive to pay a premium for reliability declines. On the values of stability to users and producers see Bruce M. Owen and Ronald Braeutigam, *The Regulation Game* (Cambridge: Ballinger, 1978).

26. Dorothy Robyn, *Braking the Special Interests: The Political Battle for Trucking Deregulation* (Ph.D. diss., 1982, University of California, Berkeley).

27. White elephants in public works are very expensive but appeal to few users. Therefore their creators constantly coerce or cajole new users to use an inappropriate facility to cover the facilities' sunk costs. For example, some argue that the Integrated System Digital Networks (ISDN) being developed in Europe will do everything poorly and at great expense. They contend that it would be wiser to let the market determine winning and losing services. If Europe spends billions on ISDN, however, it is unlikely to abandon the project quickly, even if inefficient. See also Peter Cowhey, Jonathan Aronson, Joseph Markoski, and Thomas Ramsey, "The Dilemmas of Regulating the Telematics Market in the Third World," paper presented to the Annual Meeting of the American Society for Public Administration, 1983.

28. *U.S. National Study*, p. 95.

29. For a description of the so-called Nordtel case, see Geza Feketekuty and Jonathan David Aronson, "Restrictions on Trade in Communication and Information Services," *The Information Society*, vol. 2, nos. 3/4, 1984, p. 240.

30. The case that raised this concern involved PACNET, a subsidiary of a British firm, which applied for a license to conduct international business from American shores.

31. *U.S. National Study,* p. 89.

32. Ibid., p. 71.

33. This statement assumes that the country does not have such a discount that it is extremely short-sighted. Occasionally a desperate ruling party in an OECD nation may fit this mold because of political circumstances, and certainly some developing countries have very high discount rates.

34. Even if enlisting the support of several nations is possible, it will take longer to build comparable levels of confidence this way; and the estimates of odds are what matter in calculations of discounted present value.

35. Robert O. Keohane, "The Demand for International Regimes," *International Organization,* vol. 36, no. 2 (Spring 1982), pp. 325–56.

36. In fact, to encourage reconstruction, the United States often allowed others' imports a better deal than they demanded for U.S. exports. The United States tolerated some of the protectionist policies required to build the European Community. It also limited U.S. trade and investment access to the Japanese market to allow the Japanese to get back on their feet.

37. We are not claiming that the United States has lost its power. It remains, of course, the most important economic entity in the world. We are only saying that the relative power and influence of the United States has declined as other industrial countries have bounced back and as developing countries have made progress.

38. John Gerard Ruggie, "International Regimes, Transactions, and Change: Embedded Liberalism in the Postwar Economic Order," *International Organization,* vol. 36, no. 2 (Spring 1982), pp. 379–416.

39. Miriam Camps and William Diebold, Jr., *The New Multilateralism: Can the World Trading System Be Saved?* (New York: Council on Foreign Relations, 1983).

40. Peter F. Cowhey and Edward Long, "Testing Theories of Regime Change: Hegemonic Decline or Surplus Capacity?" *International Organization,* vol. 37, no. 2 (Spring 1983), pp. 157–88.

41. It is significant, for instance, that members of the European Community have been willing to cede responsibility for their trade negotiations to the community but have retained total control over international monetary and financial authority.

42. Robert E. Baldwin and T. Scott Thompson, "Responding to Trade-Distorting Policies of Other Countries," *American Economic Review,* vol. 74, no. 2 (May 1984), pp. 270–76.

43. Recent talks between the United States and Canada about liberalizing trade flows for data services have tentatively embraced this principle.

44. Sizing is not incompatible with three ideas that have circulated in international trade circles. There might be "a 'GATT plus' embracing nations prepared to trade on a freer basis than that agreed in the GATT. Second, a 'super-GATT' to unite a group of nations which would exercise trade leadership towards a more liberal system. Third, a 'GATT of the like-minded' where

some countries would lower barriers and invite other nations to join them." All three approaches, as we understand them, differ from the concept of strict reciprocity that we next discuss. "U.K. Government Doubtful over Plans to Reform GATT, *Financial Times* (March 18, 1983), p. 6.

45. A good case on behalf of reciprocity is found in Judith L. Goldstein and Stephen D. Krasner, "Unfair Trade Practices: The Case for a Differential Response," *American Economic Review*, vol. 74, no. 2 (May 1984), pp. 283–87. Baldwin and Thompson criticize the idea in "Responding."

www.ingramcontent.com/pod-product-compliance
Lightning Source LLC
Jackson TN
JSHW061756151224
75386JS00041BA/1547